IN A NUTSHELL

THE STORY OF
KENTISH COBNUTS

✶✶✶

MEG GAME

ILLUSTRATIONS BY
CHRIS HOWKINS

Published by
Chris Howkins

COPYRIGHT
© Text Meg Game 1999
© Illustrations Chris Howkins 1999

PUBLISHER
Chris Howkins, 70 Grange Road,
New Haw, Addlestone, Surrey,
KT15 3RH

PRINTED
Unwin Brothers Ltd., The Gresham Press,
Old Woking, Surrey, England.
GU22 9LH

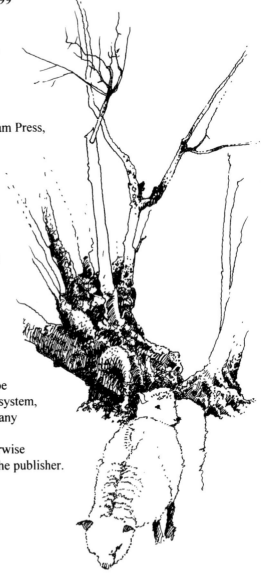

ISBN 1 901087 15 8

CONTENTS

Acknowledgements

Many people helped me to research and write this book. Thanks are most particularly due to John Cannon, Tim Chambers, Inês Ferreira, Vivien Gainsborough Foot, Gillian Jones, Pam Jordan, Graham Myers, Rachel Simpson, David Stapleton, Ian Yarham, and the staff of the Royal Horticultural Society's Lindley Library, where the majority of the historical research was carried out.

Above all, I would like to thank my brothers John and David for their continued support, and for allowing us to retain the idyllic home where we grew up together.

INTRODUCTION

In 1939 my parents, newly wed, bought a farmhouse in Kent. Soon they found themselves with hungry evacuees to feed, so they purchased the nut orchard adjoining their garden, where they could keep a pig and some ducks. In due course the pig met its appointed end, but the ducks wisely endeared themselves with various antics and died natural deaths. However, by this time my parents had discovered the delights of Kentish cobnuts, of which they now had an abundant supply.

When I was a child, my mother and I would search for wild flowers in the nut plantation, progressing to the apple, cherry and pear orchards on the neighbouring farm. The cherry orchard had to be avoided when the fruit was ripening, however, because of the terrifying bangs which erupted without warning from the bird scarers hidden beneath the towering trees. Today, alas, the landscape is different. A featureless field replaces the cherry orchard, and the present apple trees, hardly taller than I am, grow out of bare earth - no flowers here. However, our cobnut orchard remains, cherished for its old trees and the plants and animals they support, and nurtured for future generations to enjoy.

This book tells the story of cobnuts. The drawings by Chris Howkins illustrate a selection of the species associated with established nut orchards.

Changing landscapes - nut plat around an oast in Kent which was once far commoner, when hops and nuts were grown together.

Changing landscapes - nut plats have been turned over to sheep pasture where once the land was tilled and double cropped with other fruits.

Hazel Nuts, Cobnuts and Filberts

What are cobnuts?

A cobnut is a kind of hazel nut. There are cultivated forms of hazel nut, just as there are cultivated forms of apple, pear and other fruit. However, cultivated hazel nuts resemble their wild ancestors more than, say, a Bramley apple resembles a wild crab apple. Nevertheless, there are probably several hundred varieties of hazel, differing in characteristics such as taste, size and time of ripening.

Kentish Cob (or Kentish Cobnut) is one such variety, and the one planted in quantity in London's Home Counties in the 19th century. However, as Kent has traditionally been the main county producing hazel nuts, the term Kentish cobnut is often used generally to mean hazel nuts grown in England, of whatever variety.

The first cultivated hazel nuts

The The Romans developed and cultivated many kinds of fruit, and brought some to Britain during their occupation of these islands. According to Tacitus, writing nearly two thousand years ago, British soils generally produced good crops even though our climate was 'wretched, with its frequent rains and mists', and apples, plums, pears and other fruits were grown in Britain. The Romans were fond of hazel nuts, and took cultivated forms to several other occupied territories, but, although their garrisoned soldiers are known to have eaten hazels, there is no evidence to indicate whether the Romans grew cultivated varieties in Britain. It might have been easier to gather nuts from the wild woods still covering much of the island, where hazel was plentiful.

We do know that cultivated varieties of hazel were being grown in England by the mid 16th century at the latest. Cultivated hazel nuts were termed filberts, distinguishing them from wild hazels or 'small nuts'. Peter Trueris, who wrote *The Grete Herball* in 1526, seemed dubious, however, that cultivated filberts were better than wild hazels, although it is difficult to divine his full meaning. In 1526 he wrote that filberts *'ben colder than hasyll nottes / theye savour is more pontyke / and hevy / and more tycher than the small nottes be and ben of slower dygestyon and ben later of the yssue out of the body.'* However, he recommends using filberts medicinally: *'they be profytable for them that hath the old cough / yf they be bett with hony and eaten ..... yf they be stamped with the outward huskes and the old grece of a sowe or a beare .... this will cause heere to come up in the balde places'.* You would surely need to be desperate to spread your pate with such a smelly concoction.

In 1573 Tusser recommended red and white 'filbeardes' for growing in the garden. These two kinds are very similar, differing largely in the colour of the skin covering the nut. They are still available today, though no longer widely grown. At about the same time Heresbachius wrote that filberts *'delighteth in claie and waterishe groundes and upon hilles, beeing well able to abide the cold'.*

Twenty-five years later John Gerard illustrated three kinds of hazel nut in his famous *Herbal*: a 'Filberd', a 'Wild Hedge Nut' and a 'Filberd Nut of Constantinople'. The filbert (as it is spelled today) is depicted as a pointed nut with a long, tubular husk totally enclosing the nut; it was, Gerard said, grown in gardens and orchards. The wild hedge nut was so well known it *'needeth not any description'.* It commonly grew in *'woods and dankish, untoiled places',* but there were sundry sorts, varying in shape, size and date of ripening, and including one *'that is manured in our gardens, which is very great, bigger than any Filberd, and yet a kind of Hedge Nut'.* The 'Filberd Nut of Constantinople' is illustrated as a squat nut set in a short, spiky husk.

His illustrations help confirm the identity of these nuts. The 'Wild Hedge Nut' depicted by Gerard was evidently the native hazel which grew abundantly in the woods and hedges . The Red Filbert and White Filbert, with their very long husks, are closely related to

Corylus maxima, a species found wild in Turkey and beyond. Although quite similar to our own wild hazel, it produces nuts with husks which protrude well beyond the end of the nut and totally enclose it. Gerard's 'Filberd Nut of Constantinople' resembles the nuts of the Turkish Hazel, *Corylus colurna*. This is unusual among the genus in growing into a proper tree, and one that does not produce suckers .

In 1629 Parkinson stated that he had obtained nuts from Virginia, but did not know if anyone was growing them. Two species of hazel are found in eastern North America, but both bear small nuts set in long husks, so it seems unlikely that either was used for breeding cultivated forms. But who knows? Only a careful genetic study could unravel the ancestry of the myriad cultivated hazels available today.

The development of new varieties

As the 17th, 18th and early 19th centuries progressed, more hazel varieties are listed in fruit manuals and catalogues, every original author presenting a different set of names and recommendations. Of course some varieties had more than one name, and no doubt there were many local varieties too which never made it into the reference books. Most early writers retained the distinction between filberts, with long husks obscuring the fruit, and other hazel nuts. Probably the first illustration of a nut labelled as a 'cob' was drawn in 1727; it shows a nut with a husk which protrudes a little way beyond the nut, but open at the end, not contracted like that of a filbert. All the same, filberts were considered to be the choicest varieties, and were 'brought to the best tables for dessert'.

The 19th century saw great interest in breeding new varieties of plants. Many apples, pears and other fruits were developed, some of which are still in cultivation today. Hazel nuts were no exception. At the start of the 20th century, catalogues described only half a dozen or so varieties, whereas a few years earlier Hogg's *Fruit Manual* of 1884 names 30 different types of filberts and cobnuts. Of course some of these may have been synonyms since there was no standardisation or trialling of varieties in those days, and confusion reigned. Much was done to sort out the situation by a German called Goeschke, who in 1887 published a treatise on hazel nuts. It is some 200 pages long and illustrates and describes in detail about 70 varieties which he considered distinct, complete with their synonyms - what a work of analytical skill and patience.

To give some idea of the multiplication of names, take for example the variety we call Red Filbert today (which has green leaves, and is not to be confused with the purple-leaved Purple Filbert). Goeschke named it Rote Lambertsnuss, and then listed all the following as synonyms, (but some still need clarifying to this day):

Augustnuss
Aveline rouge longue
Avelinier
Avelinier rouge
Avellane franche
Bartnuss
Bluthaselnuss
Blutnuss
Franche rouge
Gemeine rote Lambertsnuss
Gros Aveline rouge
Gross Précose de Frauendorf
Haselnuss mit roter Frucht
Red Filbert
Red Hazel
Red Kernel Filbert
Red Skinned Filbert
Rotnuss
Röhrige Haselnuss
Rote Lampertusnuss
Rotkernige Zellernuss

Rouge d'Alger
Ruhrnuss
Hosnnuss
Lambertsnuss
Lambertsnuss mit rotem Kern
Lange rote Lambertsnuss
Lombardische Nuss
Lombardische rote Haselnuss
Noisetier à cerneau rouge
Noisetier à fruit rouge
Noisetier Algérienne rouge
Noisetier à pellicule rouge
Noisetier bâtarde rouge
Noisetier du Piémont à fruit rouge
Noisetier du Piémontaise rouge
Noisetier franc à amande rouge
Noisetier franc à fruit rouge
Noisetier Lambertine rouge
Noisetier Piémontaise rouge
Noisetier rouge

The most important variety introduced on to the market in 19th century England was named Lambert's Filbert. It is still grown but is now known as Kentish Cob. It was developed, or conceivably imported from abroad, by a Mr Lambert, probably around 1830. He lived in the small town of Goudhurst in Kent where his splendid house survives, right opposite the parish church. Appropriately it is called *Lamberts*, although it has long since passed out of the Lambert family. The extensive garden grows an assortment of old nut trees, presumably planted by Mr Lambert, of which several are indeed the variety Kentish Cob.

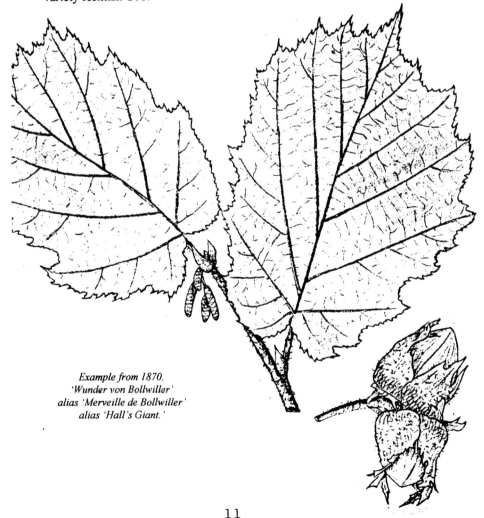

Example from 1870.
'Wunder von Bollwiller'
alias 'Merveille de Bollwiller'
alias 'Hall's Giant.'

Naming Names

Cobnut and *Filbert*

Use of the word 'cob' in connection with hazel nuts goes back many centuries. To 'cob' meant to throw lightly, and children in the 16th century used to play a game called coblenut or cob-nut. This involved pitching at a row of nuts piled in heaps; those knocked down became the property of the player. (The traditional game of conkers had to await the introduction of the horse chestnut or conker tree to England in 1616.) The nut used for pitching was called the cob.

Presumably bigger missiles conferred an advantage, so perhaps the word cob became associated with particularly large hazel nuts, and so eventually with cultivated ones. However, in some areas the name cobnut is still in use today to mean a wild hazel.

The distinction was put into print in 1729 by the nurseryman Batty Langley, in his book *Pomona*. Therein he distinguishes the 'hazel nut' as having a relatively short, deeply cut husk, while the 'cob-nut', has a husk a little longer than the nut, which is more oblong. His cobnut is therefore similar to the Kentish Cob of today.

The word 'filbert', by contrast, was reserved for pointed nuts with a very long husk which totally covered the nut and protruded, tube-like, beyond it. The name may be a corruption of 'full beard', relating to the long husk or beard. In 1629 Parkinson wrote that 'filberd' nuts were *wholly inclosed in long, thicke, rough huskes, bearded as it were at the upper ends'*. A writer in 1798 remarked that in some provincial dialects he had heard the filbert called the full-beard, and the fruits were called fullbeards, and that surely this was the origin of the name. There is another possibility. The word may originate from St Philbert's Day, listed as 20th August in the *Oxford Book of Saints*, roughly the day filberts are ripe; (St Philbert was a 7th century French monk). In 1751 the calendar was advanced by 11 days, so that 20th August before then would correspond to 31st August today, rather late for the first filberts to be ripe.

So it would seem that, originally, 'cobs' were improved varieties of our own hazel nut, with a relatively short husk, whereas 'filberts' were more closely related to the European, long-husked species. Later the popular distinction became that filberts had a husk longer than the nut, and cobs shorter. However, an 1879 article in the August *Journal of the Royal Horticultural Society*

Illus. - Mature nut orchards where the trees are grown close enough to shade out the grass provide woodland conditions as in a coppice. Snowdrops find a safe refuge in some of these orchards and provide wonderful white drifts and clumps in February when the catkins are lengthening.

complained that this was incorrect, and that hazels should be
divided as follows: filbert nuts were oblong, shaped like a
finger nail, and generally remaining in the husk; cob
nuts were shorter and broader, like a thumbnail,
rather large, with thick shells, and generally
falling from the husk.

However, this analysis was ignored, and
today we are left with the definition
being, quite arbitrarily, whether the
husk is longer or shorter than the nut.
This distinction is made all the more
meaningless by the fact that husk
length depends to some degree on
growing conditions, and is not
wholly determined by variety.
Sensibly, the Americans do not try
to make any distinction, and call all
cultivated hazel nuts 'filberts'.

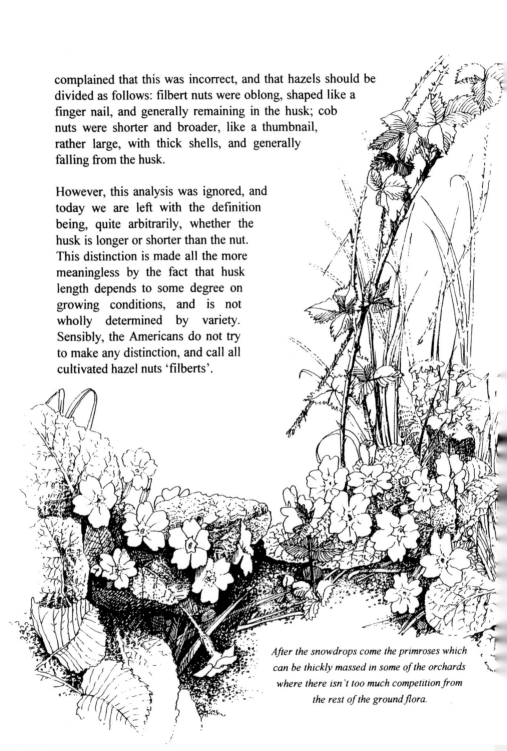

*After the snowdrops come the primroses which
can be thickly massed in some of the orchards
where there isn't too much competition from
the rest of the ground flora.*

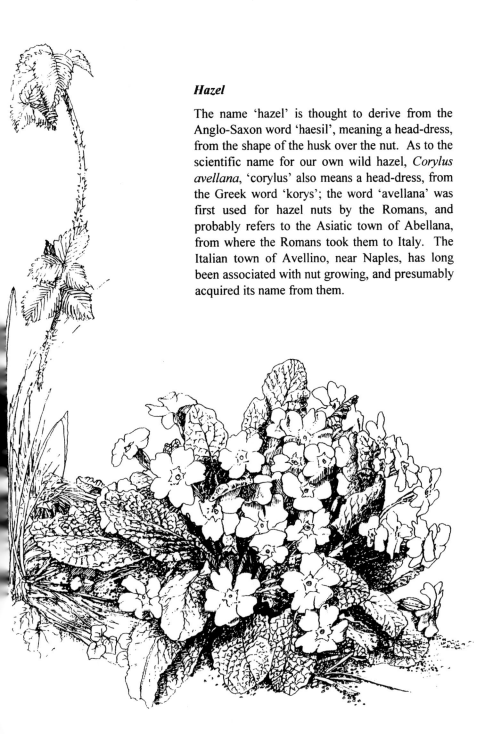

Hazel

The name 'hazel' is thought to derive from the Anglo-Saxon word 'haesil', meaning a head-dress, from the shape of the husk over the nut. As to the scientific name for our own wild hazel, *Corylus avellana*, 'corylus' also means a head-dress, from the Greek word 'korys'; the word 'avellana' was first used for hazel nuts by the Romans, and probably refers to the Asiatic town of Abellana, from where the Romans took them to Italy. The Italian town of Avellino, near Naples, has long been associated with nut growing, and presumably acquired its name from them.

Growing nuts

The beginning of commercial production

Commercial production of hazel nuts was established in Kent, and doubtless elsewhere on a smaller scale, by the late 18th century. The main variety used was White Filbert, considered to have the finest taste. There were several hundred acres of nut plantations, or 'plats', near Maidstone, and indeed it was said that there were more filberts around the county town than in all the rest of England together. Some nuts were stored for later sale; the poet John Keats, apparently a devotee, wrote to a friend on 3rd February 1818 thanking him for sending a dish of filberts, and wishing he could *'get a bucket of them by way of dessert every day for the sum of two pence. In return for your Dish of Filberts, I have gathered a few Catkins, I hope they'll look pretty.'*

Boys, in his 1796 *General View of the Agriculture of Kent*, said that the best method was to plant filberts among hops; the constant culture of the land for the hops, with the warmth and shelter they afford the young trees, caused them to grow with great luxuriance. It was also common practice to plant combinations of hops, apples, cherries and filberts together, for example 800 hop hills, 200 filbert trees and 40 apple and cherry trees to the acre.

Left - after the primroses come stunning carpets of bluebells, in orchards where the bulbs have not been disturbed for a long while. They are very tolerant of the shade. These orchard carpets are important as this is now an endangered species.

The hops might
be taken out after
a dozen years
and the filberts
after 30, by
which time the
apples and
cherries would
require the whole
space, and the
ground beneath the
trees could be put
down to grass and
grazed.

Alternatively, the filbert
trees might be retained and
the other trees removed.
Then the land could not be
grazed because the nut trees
were too small to be safely out of
reach. In this case the nuts were
inter-cropped with gooseberries, currants or other
short plants. Strawberries might even be planted between the
rows of gooseberries. A *Note* appended by 'a Middle Kent Farmer' remarked
that planting filberts and cherries together was bad practice; filberts 'answer
well on very few soils', and it was entirely owing to the skill and management
in pruning the trees, even upon a favourable soil, that they paid.

By preference, filberts were grown on relatively infertile, well-drained soil, or
'stone-shattery sandy loam'. If the soil was rich, the trees grew too
luxuriantly and produced smaller crops. A band of just such soils, derived
from the Lower Greensand, stretches east-west across the Weald of Kent to
the south of Sevenoaks and Maidstone, and on towards Ashford. This,
combined with the relative ease by which produce could be transported to the
markets of London by boat via the Medway and the Thames, made growing
nuts particularly profitable here. Filberts fetched from 16 shillings to two
pounds wholesale per hundred pounds weight in the 1790s, depending on the
size of the crop and demand. Some nuts were also sold by higglers, who
retailed them in different parts of the country.

Wild hazel nuts were also gathered in quantity from the hedges and woods and sold in the markets of London and other major towns, 'employing a great many poor families during the Autumn, who might otherwise have very little to do, and of course be a burden to the public', as William Forsyth wrote in 1806. This was not always popular with the landowner. A poster from 1812 addressed to 'Nutters' proclaimed that 'all persons found getting Nuts, and trespassing' in the Duke of Norfolk's woods 'will be prosecuted as the law directs' because a great deal of damage had been done in recent years by people 'getting nuts and breaking down and destroying Hazle wood'.

The first variety used in commercial plantations, White Filbert, is an inconsistent cropper from year to year; the nuts, though sweet and tasty, are small. Soon other varieties were being grown commercially. In 1812 Brookshaw described a nut called 'English Cob Nut' which, he said, was an exceedingly fine nut. The flavour was as good as the filbert, the shell was thin and easy to crack, and the kernel was much larger. Indeed, he continued, there was scarcely any fruit which would be a greater ornament to the dinner table. The nut was very little known, but should be more often planted, as it was a superior alternative when the filbert crop failed, which was often, and fetched a higher price.

By mid-century, the very successful variety Kentish Cob had become widely available. It is relatively reliable in the climate of southern England, producing large, tasty nuts, and was planted in quantity, even replacing White Filbert in established orchards. Most, and probably all, old orchards surviving today are predominantly of Kentish Cob, often with a thin scattering of other varieties such as White Filbert and Cosford. Kentish Cob is still planted to this day, and is a good variety for the garden.

Lesser Celandines are another spring flower of the barer patches where they can flourish ahead of summer shade.

18

Tree propagation

Cultivated hazel varieties do not come true from seed any more than a Bramley apple pip would grow into a tree producing Bramley apples. Vegetative methods, such as grafting or layering, are required to obtain a plant genetically identical to the original tree.

This was appreciated long ago; for example, advice dating from 1572 states: *'For to set filberds or hasels, and to have them good, take the small wandes that grow out from the filberd or hasell tree (with short heary twigs) and set them, and they shall bring forth as good fruit as the tree they came off'*. Using rooted suckers like this from the base of the tree remains one of the easiest ways of producing small numbers of plants. For production in quantity, today, a modified system using stool beds is used. In this method, an established plant is cut to the ground, and the resulting 'stool' is covered over with a few inches of soil or sawdust or other rooting medium. New shoots grow up the next year, and some will have formed roots by the following winter. The proportion rooting can be increased by fixing a wire round the shoot; this is called *strangling*.

Grafting is another method of producing new plants: a twig cut from a tree of the desired variety is 'grafted' onto the decapitated stem of a rooted hazel seedling. Many fruit trees, such as apples and pears, are produced by this or similar ways. However, grafting is technically difficult in

Broad-leaved Helleborine - an orchid that can flourish in the shade of some nut orchards.

19

Toothwort, Lathraea squamaria, which survives the shade by being a parasite on the nuts, taking their nutrients for itself. It therefore has no greenery of its own, but in April and May produces white or pinkish flowering spikes up to a foot high.

hazel, and today is mostly practised only by specialist nurserymen who have the right equipment. Nevertheless some of our ancestors were able to graft hazel nuts. In 1665 John Rea mentions grafting several varieties onto wild hazel stock; what he lacked of today's scientific knowledge and equipment was apparently compensated for by experience and expertise.

A third method of producing new plants is layering. Long suckers are bent over and pegged into the ground part-way along the shoot, leaving a section beyond, which is tied or propped upright. A rim of earth may be built up round the pegged section to retain water. By the following Autumn the pegged section should have rooted, and the new plant can be severed from the parent tree and taken to nursery beds to be grown on for a couple of years.

A disadvantage of grafted plants is that any suckers which grow up from the ground will be from the root stock, not from the desired variety, whereas suckers from trees produced by layering or stoolbeds are genetically identical to the main tree, and can be used to replace the original stem if necessary. This has commonly been done in many old Kentish Cobnut plats, where the original trunk has rotted away.

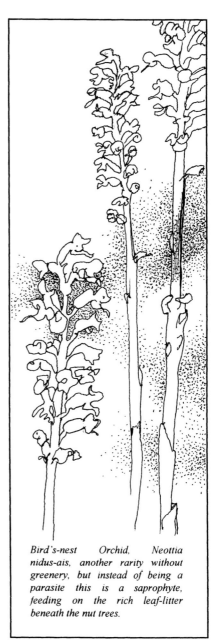

Bird's-nest Orchid, Neottia nidus-ais, another rarity without greenery, but instead of being a parasite this is a saprophyte, feeding on the rich leaf-litter beneath the nut trees.

21

Pruning, wanding and brutting

By the early 19th century, Kent not only possessed the greatest area of hazel nut orchards of any county, but had developed a very particular method of pruning trees to produce fruit of the highest quality. In 1834 John Rogers advised that, *'as respects the pruning of the filbert, the reader would not be so wise in his whole life as a visit to Maidstone would make him in one hour'*. He commented that the generality of gardeners knew little or nothing about pruning filbert trees, and that it was remarkable that this branch of the pruner's art should have been brought to perfection by the *'untaught, unlettered Kentish peasant'*, but was not followed elsewhere. The knowledge had seemingly descended from father to son for generations. How much more valuable, he goes on, is the knowledge which has been gained by practical experience compared with that from theoreticians who bury what they really know beneath a *'load of hard names and learned quotations, which only serve to puzzle rather than inform the reader'*.

The principle of the Kentish method was to check the growth of the tree, keeping it to a mere five or six feet high, within easy reach for pruning and picking. Such hard-pruned trees bore fewer nuts, but these were much larger than those produced by a free-growing tree, twenty or more feet tall. The branches were thinned out to ensure that plenty of light reached the shoots: shaded shoots make fewer flowers, and therefore a smaller crop of nuts. Although trees were kept low-growing, the branches were trained outwards to such a degree that the tree could eventually reach twenty feet in diameter. It was shaped like a bowl, open at the centre, with about eight branches radiating out from a central stem 18 inches or so high. The young branches were first trained to near horizontal, for example by using a large hoop placed within the tree, to which the shoots were tied; the lateral spread of the young tree was then assisted by always pruning to an outward-facing bud. By this means a five year old tree might extend to six or eight feet across. Eventually the branches were allowed to turn upwards to form the bowl shape.

A well-tended tree could be pruned with nothing more than a pruning knife. Old, worn-out twigs were removed, and strong growth was cut out or pulled out, leaving plenty of fresh but weaker and less vertically-growing small branches. As one person remarked, 'after the pruning, the trees look mere skeletons'. Skilled pruners could earn 3s 6d to 4s per day in 1885; the same people often pruned the gooseberries and currants and, later, superintended picking and packing the fruit.

Pruning was normally undertaken in January to March, ideally when the catkin was in flower. The catkins are the male flowers, each catkin producing millions of tiny grains of pollen; they were also known as aglets, kentice, gull, and, most descriptively, as blowings. The female flowers or 'nutkins' resemble tiny tufts of bright red bristles; to produce nuts, they must be fertilised by pollen, which is so light it is carried along by the breeze. The idea of pruning when the catkins and nutkins were out was that jogging the branches would help disperse the pollen. Growers were also recommended to tap the branches with a stick on a warm, still day, and both I and my father used to do this. However, it turns out hazel nut varieties are not self-compatible: pollen from a different variety is needed to fertilise the flowers. For example, Kentish Cob pollen cannot fertilize the female flowers of Kentish Cob. Like many old plats, mine is composed of Kentish Cob and a few White Filbert, the latter supposedly a pollinator for the former, although in fact the catkins are over far too early. Most old plats, mine included, must therefore be pollinated by seedlings in the hedges and woods, and our tapping of the branches was a useless exercise, though it was pleasant to watch the clouds of pollen drift by. Today I only tap the branches of hazels in the surrounding hedges. Modern plantations include several varieties, to ensure good pollination.

Hazel tends to produce suckers, which are called 'wands'; these thin, straight shoots do resemble the image of a fairy's wand. Spawn is another old Kentish name for them. Most come from the trunk near or just below the ground. If a branch has died, a wand can be

One of the old pruning tools.

23

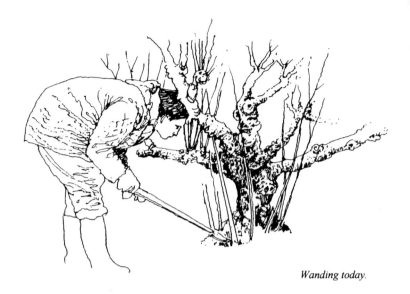

Wanding today.

trained to replace it. Otherwise all wands must be removed annually, a job which could be carried out by an unskilled labourer, without taking up the time of the practised pruner. Many wands could be removed using a wanding iron - a tool resembling a large chisel on a five or six foot wooden handle, which has gone out of use today. The blade was aimed downwards at the brittle junction of the wand and the trunk: if a wand is torn off from the base like this, it is less likely to re-sprout the following year. Unfortunately shoots from below ground have to be cut out separately, a back-breaking job. Sometimes the roots of the tree were laid bare for some distance from the bole for a period in winter, and all vestiges of suckers removed; they might then be covered up again with manure, small prunings or leaves.

The wands themselves had various uses; farmers employed them for 'splints', sprung crosswise on the top of baskets of fruit to keep down the paper or hay with which they were covered, and baskets made from them were used by coal miners. The tips were used for staking small pot plants. My father tried selling bundles for pea sticks, but their volume made this uneconomic. Today, sadly, wands and other small prunings are either burnt or are chipped and spread on the ground, small numbers only being retained for use in the garden. They are too small for hurdles.

The third pruning operation was 'brutting', carried out in July or August. This entailed breaking strong, upwardly-growing shoots, especially those near the top of the trees, about half way along their length; sap exuded from the break, which reduced secondary growth. The broken section was left dangling, to be removed later during the winter pruning. The idea was to 'ripen the wood' and to reduce the summer growth of unwanted shoots.

24

Digging and manuring

It seems incredible today, but nut orchards were dug every year. The object was to remove weeds and to expose the larvae of the nut weevil, a troublesome pest, to the frost.

Digging was carried out using a three-pronged plat fork or 'spud', and a whole layer of soil was moved by inverting each forkful in large clods, leaving it to be broken down by the winter frosts. It was paid by piece-work, so labourers might be tempted to miss out areas, covering up undug ground by throwing soil on top of it; the wary overseer would probe suspect soil with a stick before paying the workmen. Early this century piece-rates were £1- £2 per acre, or an old penny a tree. Further cultivation during the season was carried out with a hoe, and some orchards were maintained virtually weed-free year-round.

Nut plats were also regularly manured, a variety of materials being brought in by train, or barge if the farm was near the Medway. Waste from the wool mills and old rags might be used, or fish waste, which cannot have been popular with the neighbours. Feathers were available in plenty after Christmas. One current grower used turkey feathers until the 1980s; the ground was covered with the white down for such a long time that a friend visiting in June mistook it for an extremely late snowfall. Farmyard manure might be employed, either from the farm itself or brought in from London, where numerous horses were stabled. However, it was not generally popular as, being heavy, it was difficult and therefore expensive to spread beneath trees; it was also thought to be too rich.

All this labour of course required a commensurate workforce. Today labour is not so cheap, and growers have turned to more economical means of managing the vegetation beneath the trees. Most people use mowing machines, but some have turned to sheep or even to geese; elderly birds are said to be the best as they have learnt how to deal with foxes. As a young girl I was terrorised on my return home from school by the flock of geese in our neighbour's nut plantation, which delighted in rushing over to hiss at me through the fence.

25

Picking the nuts

Nuts can be marketed at various stages of their development. The first opportunity arises when the kernels have filled up the shells, which is usually in mid to late August in the south of England. Some people prefer cobnuts at this stage, when the husks and shells are still green. The kernels are crisp and juicy, and the flavour can be enhanced with a little salt. The nuts are still firmly attached to the branch, but an experienced worker picks quickly by breaking a joint in the stalk with the thumb. These nuts may fetch a high price right at the start of the season, especially as they weigh heavy, being full of moisture. They keep only a week or so in this prime condition and therefore need to be sold and consumed promptly.

About a month later the nuts are ripe, and the trees are picked again. A brisk shake of the branches brings the bunches tumbling down, and they are gathered from the ground - another back-breaking task. The husks and shells are a beautiful golden colour, but gradually darken to a deep brown, making them look less attractive than the green nuts. In these days of pre-washed, pre-wrapped produce, sales tend to fall off at this stage - a great shame as the kernels are now at their tastiest, and keep well too. If prices remain high, the plat may be gone over a third time, by groping through the fallen leaves as late as November to search for the last few nuts, a wet, chilly job. An average total crop is about a thousand pounds weight per acre, although it varies considerably from year to year.

Nutting was once one of the great British folk harvests, now confined largely to blackberries and bilberries.

The three pickings were traditionally called firsting, seconding and thirding. The piecework rates normally increased progressively, as fewer nuts were left at each stage. If the same gang of workers was allowed to pick the same area at each stage, care had to be taken by the foremen that they did not 'accidentally' leave a good many nuts behind at the firsting, so that they could obtain the maximum from the higher rates the second time round. One solution

26

was to recruit a gang of casual pickers at short notice, whereupon the 'regulars' saw their investment disappear. A few growers sold their crop on the tree, as they had their hops to attend to, and did not want the trouble of picking and selling nuts at the busiest time of the year.

Local papers of the 19th century reported dozens of disputes, brawls and petty thefts concerning hop pickers but nut pickers seem to have been less troublesome; most of them were probably local folk. Nevertheless a few thefts were recorded, such as the man who was sentenced to six weeks' hard labour for stealing 33 pounds of cobnuts from a farm near Mereworth. In court he said he was very sorry, and "it was all through drink or he would not have done it". Another thief, in 1875, was given the option of either a fine of £3 plus 16s 6d costs, or two months' hard labour. He had stolen 19 pounds of cobnuts and some apples, together worth 7s 6d, from Mr Frank Day at East Farleigh. His descendants are still farming cobnuts.

Whole families took part in the picking so that after the development of compulsory education schools granted a day's closure for nutting.

Traditionally the nuts were picked into wicker baskets called *kipsies*, but when I was a girl we picked into hessian sacks. These were fastened to our waists, like aprons, by string tied round potatoes in the top corners of the sack. Since my father was a busy man, the trees in our small plantation had grown up beyond the orthodox six feet or so. This meant we younger pickers had to scramble up into the branches but at least the bowl shape of the tree was easy to climb and stand in. The nuts in our 'aprons' were turned out periodically into a larger sack. At this time leaves and any other debris were removed. I remember when I was very young one of our regular pickers

27

would add some nuts to my paltry collection so I would not be teased by my older brothers (not that it seemed to make much difference to their behaviour). When full, or at the end of the day, each picker's sack was carted off to be checked and weighed. There were complaints if too many leaves, bad nuts and other unwanted material was included. Shortly before the War the rate for picking was as little as 6d for a 20 pounds basket. In the 1950s my father paid about 2d a pound. Today the rate is around 20p a pound. Occasionally two nutshells become inextricably joined in growth, like Siamese twins. The nut pickers of my childhood always regarded these as lucky charms, and kept them. Naturally *I'm* not in the least superstitious - but I too keep them, or give them to out-of-luck friends.

In the 1960s and 70s, I sometimes helped my father with the sorting and packing. Quite a few red or yellow ladybirds had usually climbed to the top of the sacking, and I would carefully pick them off and let them go in the garden. It was a different story with the earwigs, which always accumulated at the bottom of the sack. I hated earwigs, so someone else had to sort through the last few nuts. Eventually I decided that this irrational fear was too inconvenient for a nut grower, and gradually conditioned myself to them; today I can handle them with no more than slight unease.

The annual nut harvest was followed by a special 'Crack-nut Sunday' service of thanksgiving.

28

Marketing the crop

Nuts used to be sent to market in 'sieves'. These were round baskets about a foot in depth and one and a half feet in diameter, often made from osiers. A sieve held about 28 pounds of green nuts or 40 pounds of ripe ones; smaller ones held half this amount. Large sacks holding 50 pounds or more were also used; the open end was sewn up with a large bodkin and string. Prices in the 1880s ranged from 5d to 1s 4d per pound, depending partly on the quantity of imported nuts of various kinds. David Stapleton, a former grower in West Peckham, remembers half sieve baskets fetching £1 about 50 years ago. You had to pack the nuts down hard to fit the requisite 20 pounds into the basket, and some people resorted to placing a sack over the nuts, climbing on top, and treading them down with hobnailed boots. The sieves were covered with paper pegged down with small wands or cleft sticks. Mr Stapleton and his father put a round piece of blue tissue paper over the nuts, and then a layer of green bracken; this was secured with three or four wands cut a little longer than the width of the basket, with a taper at each end, which were thrust through the sides of the basket to hold everything in place. After his father died, Mr Stapleton tried using bracken he had cut the previous week, but Pouparts, the agents, almost refused to buy the consignment as the browning bracken suggested the nuts were not fresh.

The bulk of the Kentish crop was despatched to the markets in London at Borough, Spitalfields, Farringdon and, of course, Covent Garden - not the new site at Nine Elms, but the old market in the heart of town. In the 19th century, transport was either by water or, later, by railway. Railway stations in the heart of the fruit-growing areas were the scene of great bustle at the end of the day in the fruit season. Heavily laden carts or 'fruit-vans' came in from all directions, piled high with baskets of fruit or barrels of apples. There was much jostling as their drivers were anxious to deliver their burden and get home. The fruit-vans, a peculiarity of Kent, were light trolleys set on narrow-tyred wheels, and sprung. The sides and back were made of open lattice-work just fine enough to retain the baskets, and about four feet high, so that they could carry several layers of sieves or barrels. There were complaints that the Kentish railway companies carried the produce by slow luggage trains, and overcharged; it was said that it cost as much to convey fruit 40 miles to London as to bring it from Normandy.

In my father's day, nuts were packed into recycled wooden Dutch tomato trays which, with a bit of push and shove, just held ten pounds. A brown paper cover was stapled over the top, and my father used to pay me a few pence to inscribe these with our name and address until, no longer requiring the income, I purchased him a rubber stamp. The packed nuts were taken to a nearby depot (usually un-staffed) for collection by a haulier, and the grower left a scrap of paper sandwiched between the boxes listing his name and the number of boxes. This seemed, even then, an astonishingly casual arrangement, but I do not recall any disputes.

Storage

Cobnuts can be stored quite well for months in the right conditions. They are seeds, after all, and in the ground must be able to resist rot until they germinate. The ideal store will mimic cool winter conditions. If the nuts get too wet they go mouldy; if too dry, the kernels wither and then, though still tasty, they do not possess that wholesome crunchiness which is the hallmark of a good fresh cobnut.

Today the best place to keep them is in the fridge or a cold store, but of course this was not available to previous generations. Methods then included covering them with dry sand and putting them in a jar or an earthenware pot. A suggestion from 1572 was to '*put them in a pot with hony, and they shall continue fresh a yeare, and the sayd hony will be gentle and good for many medicines*'. You can buy hazel nuts in honey as a delicacy on the Continent today, though the nuts are chewy, not at all like fresh cobnuts. In 1816 the Horticultural Society was presented with some nuts which had been kept fresh for eighteen months in a butter firkin in a cellar; '*the pores of the wood having been completely stopped by the butter, the external air is prevented from passing through them ..... the moisture, arising from the salt in the butter, which has penetrated into the wood, also contributes.*'

The most regular method of keeping nuts, used since at least the 17th century (and perhaps as far back as the beginning of pottery), was in a pot buried in the ground; this was said to keep the nuts 'moist and sweete until new come'. Gardeners on Victorian estates had to develop effective means of storing large quantities, and this became a subject of debate in the *Gardener's Chronicle* in the 1880s. One man recommended keeping dry nuts in large flower pots, the bottom and top covered by slates, buried eight or nine inches in the soil, with a small stake marking the location. He reported that the 1875 crop was stored in this fashion, and he '*sent the last dishes of those nuts in for dessert (beautiful and plump) in the last week of November 1876, and they were pronounced by my employer's guests as excellent. The hot weather of July 1876 did not affect them in the least, although they were on an open border in the kitchen garden, the ground being exposed to the sun from morn to eve.*' One wonders why they stored the nuts beyond the following season, but perhaps the crop that year failed. Another man stored his cobnuts in a similar fashion but in what he termed his nut vaults, which were pits lined with dry bricks placed closely together to prevent mice getting through. The recommended position of the vaults was extraordinarily exacting, being in the east portion of a south and east angle border under the shelter of a wall. The nuts were put in dry, but with their husks on, and a sprinkling of salt was added. They were taken out as required, 'say sufficient for three or four days at a time'.

Burying nuts in a tin was a favourite method earlier this century. A few years ago a neighbour of mine was digging the garden of her newly-acquired house when her fork struck something solid. Up came a Crawford's Rover Assorted biscuit tin, very rusty and dilapidated. She recalled that, twenty or thirty years ago, people bought gold Kruger Rands and buried them for safe keeping, so she thought she had discovered a fortune. But alas, when she ripped open the lid she found the tin to be stuffed with no more than ancient cobnuts.

Commercial growers kept much larger quantities; some might be kept back for the Christmas trade, and well into the following year, even till Easter. They were typically laid up in a mouse-proof shed and turned with shovels, with salt again perhaps being added. At one Kentish farm in the 1950s and 60s cobnuts were laid about two feet deep in a cold dry cellar and were turned with shovels once a month or so. If the temperature rose too high, the nuts would sprout and have to be thrown away. Today, cold storage is used. Mice were not the only nut thieves. A man recently told me that his father kept a supply of cobnuts locked in a cupboard to protect them from his children.

A Portrait of an Old Plat

A few years ago, when I was researching the (then) decline of the nut industry, I noticed something odd about the figures for Shipbourne Parish, Kent. Between 1944 and 1951, the acreage of *old* nut plats increased! Well, it just shows you shouldn't put too much faith in statistics, I thought, but in a manner of speaking they were right - the acreage of old trees did, apparently, increase. During the War the nut trees in Silverhill Plantation were cut to the ground preparatory to clearing the land for more productive crops but the project was abandoned, the stumps were never extracted, and the trees re-grew.

After the War the land was bought by the father of the present owner. She remembers, as a girl of 12, hacking a path through the thicket to discover what they had just acquired. Over the years the family lovingly restored the jungle to a well-maintained, productive nut plat, which Pam and her late husband have maintained as part of a smallholding.

The orchard is on clay, and the trees are mostly Kentish Cob, although a few other varieties, possibly of seedling origin, are present. The trees were very close together, a situation made worse by the presence of numerous plums and apples; many of these were eventually removed, together with some of the nut trees, to make access easier.

Before the War the plat had been dug to keep down the weeds and weevils. Diggers were paid at the rate of an old penny for each tree cleared. However, once the brambles had been cleared, Pam's father decided to give up cultivation and mow the grass that grew there instead. He did continue to cultivate the ground at his other large plat nearby. Pam hoed this plantation regularly with her mother and another woman, plus two elderly men. It could be hot, hard work. Later, a local man, Billy Levitt, used to cultivate between the rows with a Howard Jem cultivator, which he would talk to all the while like a horse. He and another man pruned the plat beautifully, reducing every tree to the same height. It was said that if you spread a tablecloth over the top of a well-pruned plat then the cloth would be level.

Eventually Pam's parents moved out from the main house in favour of their daughter and her husband Tim. He had a job in London which meant mowing was difficult to fit in, so they decided to try sheep. To begin with they bought ten Romney Marsh sheep, but these proved too large, browsing the lower branches as well as the grass. My own parents' solution to this same problem was to acquire ancient ewes otherwise destined for mutton; these were less agile at getting the nut branches and their teeth were too worn down for such food. Pam and Tim had the better idea of switching to Southdown sheep, a much smaller 'Rare Breed' which Pam has to this day. The sheep are shared with another nut-grower, so the orchards can be rested. Some of the lambs go for breeding and others for meat. Pam has no problem selling the meat, but as she gets fond of the lambs she sometimes stores joints for her own use in the freezer until memory of individual animals has faded.

Pruning is now undertaken by Fred and Joan Bromley, a couple in their seventies who have been involved in the industry most of their lives. No fertilisers or sprays are used, although the sheep are wormed and vaccinated, and given antibiotics when ill. The plat rises up each side of a small stream, and the wealth of primroses and other flowers make it one of the prettiest of all nut plats.

Southdown Sheep in the nut plat: one of many old breeds that are finding a new role in sustainable conservation measures.

Richard Webb - Nut-breeder Extraordinaire

Richard Webb was an enthusiastic but eccentric nut grower of the 19th century who bred several useful new varieties. His 12 acre garden near Reading was completely enclosed by a six foot wall, setting it in a world apart. Even the gate, where visitors had to peal an enormous bell, was almost obscured by a canopy of ivy.

Most of his land was taken up with nut trees, but room was also found for figs, apricots, pears and other fruit. Mr Webb did not believe in pruning, so the garden became an exuberant thicket. The 'Black Hamburgh' grape vine, thought to be the largest in England, produced a ton of fruit annually; the length of its branches combined measured about 1,600 feet. Just one of his cobnut trees took six people a quarter of a day to gather its harvest of 110 pounds of nuts. A glorious rose, 'Marechal Niel', made its way into a greenhouse and clambered over an outbuilding, prompting one visitor to question whether it was even confined to a single county.

Mr Webb's mulberries were said to be particularly red and juicy, possibly because the tree had spread roots into a pit where he had emptied a considerable collection of wine, beer and spirits. Over the top of the pit he erected an obelisk bearing the inscription: 'To the execrated memory of alcohol', followed by two verses of doggerel beginning *'Beneath this stone lies Our nation's deadliest foe: Myriads he has hurried Down to the realms of woe'*. A table laden with fruit and cakes was kept ready for the many

visitors to the garden, but guests were never offered alcoholic drinks, having to be content with just water.

To guard his fruit from thieving birds and mice, Mr Webb kept a flock of cats, estimated at one time to number about 60. Protection from humans was afforded by half-a-dozen mastiffs with 'bloodshot eyes and murderous fangs' and, though all reputedly favourites of their master, 'a man of much kindness'.

Webb's Memorial to Alcohol

Richard Webb's House

He became well-known among the contemporary gardening fraternity and, in his later years, was visited by that famous garden designer, Gertrude Jekyll. Her memory of the meeting was so vivid that even twenty six years later she included an account of it in her book *Wood and Garden*. She reported being welcomed by a brawny, sunburnt forewoman who looked as though she could do the work of two men. Mr Webb, a Quaker, was dressed all in black. Alleys of nut trees stretched away into the distance in all directions. Miss Jekyll was enchanted and remarked that it was the only nursery she had visited where one could expect to see fairies on a summer's night.

Richard Webb produced many new hazel nut cultivars, most of them similar to Kentish Cob. He exhibited regularly at the Crystal Palace, and called his new nuts after prominent people of the day, such as Empress Eugenie, Princess Royal, Garibaldi and The Shah. 'Daviana', named after Sir Humphry Davy, became a major pollinating variety in the plantations in Oregon and has only recently been replaced by more modern cultivars. 'Garibaldi' and the eponymous 'Webb's Prize Cob' were recommended by the Ministry of Agriculture in 1937, and the latter is still quite widely available. Mr Webb thought growing hazel nuts so lucrative that he reported that no other crop would produce such an income, and that, 'compared with land for building purposes, it would yield 10 times the profit.'

Mr Webb's fruit and nut diet and abstinence from alcohol served him well, for he lived to be 79 and was hale and hearty almost to the end. His house and garden were sold by auction the following year, 1878; some of his varieties continued to be promoted by his son-in-law, T. O. Cooper.

Intrigued by the story of Richard Webb, I wondered if any of the gardens had survived. Research in the British Museum Map Room suggested that it had succumbed to an extensive modern housing estate. In the hope that traces might yet remain, one day I set off, none too hopefully, to Reading.

After searching the estate diligently but unsuccessfully, I was ready to depart when I spied a high, old wall with several nut trees peeping over the top. The old garden had been divided among several exclusive houses, (Mr Webb's calculations of the relative values of orchard and building land having eventually proved quite erroneous), but his house, some of the nut trees, and his monument to alcohol (or rather to its abstinence) were still there. Had I arrived just a fortnight earlier, I could have explored several acres of his nut walks but these had just been cleared for further house-building. More of his trees can still be found in the grounds of a local radio station, in a building appropriately named 'The Filberts'.

The Rise and Fall of the Nut Industry

'Is it not rather surprising, when we see all the world so fond of cracking nuts after dinner, that the cultivation of British nuts is so generally neglected?...Surely a dish of fine filberts in the husk is more ornamental in the dessert, and much less unwholesome, than the dried foreign nuts of the shops, which, in order to give them a bright outside appearance, have been half roasted, perhaps half a dozen times.'

This comment of 1841 is still all too appropriate today, when so much produce is imported, and appearance is considered more important than taste.

Perhaps the complaint was heeded then, for cobnut cultivation seems to have expanded to a thriving business by the end of the 19th century. Whitehead, in his detailed study of fruit farming in Kent of 1885, thought growing nuts a most profitable enterprise and was surprised that more land in Kent suited for it had not been planted with filbert or cobnut trees. He blamed landlords for not helping tenants with the start-up costs, which were high, as it took twelve to fifteen years for nuts to come into full bearing.

An agricultural census in 1913 estimated the national area of cobnuts at 7,325 acres, of which the bulk was undoubtedly in Kent. This was probably the period when the acreage planted with nuts was at its maximum. A relentless decline followed the Great War so that by 1936 the estimated national area had shrunk to 1,855 acres, with Kent contributing 1,385 acres. At this date the parish of Plaxtol in Kent had the most at 120 acres. It was closely followed by Ightham at 109 and East Farleigh at 104. Other counties listed included Gloucestershire at 71 acres, Worcestershire at 56, Surrey at 38 and Buckinghamshire at 36.

The 1944 estimate was down to 1,230 acres in Kent, which had fallen to 730 in 1951. After this, cobnuts were no longer thought to be worth including in the national statistics. By 1990 the area in Kent was in the region of 200-250 acres, including plats so derelict that most people would not have recognised them as such.

The reasons for this decline were several. Home produce had to compete with imported fruits and nuts, which became increasingly available due to improvements in transport and refrigeration. Better methods of treatment, such as roasting, salting and, later, vacuum packaging, kept the foreign nuts in prime condition during their journey. Their transport costs were reduced once the nuts could be shelled and processed in the country of origin. As early as 1896 a salesman advised British growers that the demand for stored cobnuts was falling away. No doubt they had to compete with almonds and other imports. He advised British growers to market more of their produce fresh and in season. There was also a fall in demand from aboard ships. Cobnuts had always been

much in demand as one of the few foodstuffs which could be kept fresh throughout the voyage. Now this market declined as it became increasingly possible to preserve other fresh foods for such journeys.

Nuts had been profitable on relatively infertile land but as fertilisers and pesticides became more generally available, so it became increasingly profitable to grow other crops. Strawberries, raspberries and apples were prime among these. Cobnut cultivation is labour intensive and difficult to mechanise on a small scale, so as wages rose so too did the costs of nut production. They became one of the most expensive tree crops to grow according to a Ministry of Agriculture *Bulletin* of 1937. It quoted a figure of £12 16s (£12.80) as the typical annual costs per acre and that excluded picking and marketing. The breakdown of this was given as follows:

land charge	£2 0s (£2.00)
digging	£2 10s (£2.50)
hoeing	£1 16s (£1.80)
pruning	£2 0s (£2.00)
brutting	£0 10s (£0.50)
spraying	£0 10s (£0.50)
fertilisers	£3 10s (£3.50)

Thus the jobs which had to be done by hand - digging, hoeing, pruning and brutting - accounted for just over half the total. The fertiliser recommended was the application of 20-30 hundredweight per acre of organic manures annually, plus 10-15 hundredweight of lime every three to four years. Again, much of the cost of this must have been the labour of spreading it. (Incidentally, the spray recommended was lead arsenate, not a substance anyone would dream of using today!)

The Ministry of Agriculture *Bulletin* also noted that '*pruning is an expert operation and is often a hereditary craft in the villages near Maidstone, but skilled cutters are not so common as they once were*', and thought this a reason that nut cultivation was '*not so much extending in spite of the generally profitable character of the industry*'.

The Second World War caused the demise of some nut plats, either through neglect or because they were taken up to grow higher yielding crops such as potatoes. Many plats were grubbed at the command of the War Agricultural Committee, which had powers to direct what crops were grown, and could even take land away from farmers in extreme cases. The expansion of Maidstone and other towns and villages took their toll too. A post-war brochure on Maidstone remarked that a number of cobnut trees were preserved in private gardens where urban expansion had overrun former nut growing areas. A similar effect can be seen today in villages in the heart of the Kentish nut growing area, such as Plaxtol and Ightham, and infilling continues the attrition. Very few new orchards were planted after the War, with one exception of a fruit-farmer in East Sussex, whose principal motivation for choosing cobnuts was that they were almost the only crop not subject to government regulation. Plats have also been lost through long-term neglect, and (especially recently) removal for horse pasture or garden expansion.

Cobnuts and Nature Conservation

Old Kentish cobnut plantations make an important contribution to nature conservation. A century ago, the plants and animals that nut plats support might have been quite common in the surrounding woods, hedges and fields. Modern monocultures of strictly-controlled intensive agriculture provide no such havens. By contrast, the management of many nut plats today has generally become less intensive than formerly; the regular digging and hoeing used for weed control has been often replaced with mowing or grazing, to the benefit of the flora and fauna.

Dormice

Rachel Simpson, a Kentish nut grower, went out one day to the greenhouse on the edge of her nut plat to feed her cat. She picked up an opened tin of catfood and out jumped a dormouse. it was lucky not to become cat food itself. She put it back in the orchard with a supply of nuts.

Rachel was fortunate to see this animal, for dormice are extremely hard to watch in the wild. They are active at night, foraging in the branches of trees and shrubs in search of their wide range of food, including nuts, berries, insects, and the flowers of hawthorn and honeysuckle. In early autumn they feast on hazel nuts, which are important to their survival, being very nutritious and just what they need to build up body fat for the approaching six months of hibernation. This they spend in hideaways near the ground, where the temperature is relatively constant; the boles of old nut trees are riddled with nooks and crannies, and I imagine that dormice living in nut plats are spoilt for choice for their winter quarters. Although their body temperature may fall to near freezing during this period, they still use up energy just keeping alive, and may only weigh half as much at the end as at the beginning. Lewis Carroll's depiction of a sleepy dormouse in *Alice's Adventures in Wonderland* was appropriate, for not only do they spend half the year in hibernation, but they also go into torpor during the rest of the year in cold spells or when food is short. They make up for this inactive time by living for up to five years, much longer than most other mammals of similar size.

Dormice eat hazel nuts at the start of the season, when the shells are still soft and the nuts are firmly attached to the branch. They very rarely go down to the ground, so if a nut they are opening falls off, they just have to begin again with another. They open nuts by scooping out a neat circular hole in one side, leaving tooth marks going round and round the hole rather than across the flat face. One way to detect the presence of dormice is to look for these characteristically chewed nuts, and this is how I discovered they live in my own nut plat, although it took a while to find just one single nut among the myriad empty shells of those taken by nuthatches, grey squirrels, voles, foxes and other animals.

It typically takes a dormouse about 20 minutes to open a wild hazel nut, but cobnuts, being larger and thicker shelled, may take longer. However, they find a feast - a dormouse weighs only five or six times the kernel of a good-sized cobnut. They have now been found in quite a few cobnut plats, and it seems they are quite at home in nutteries, especially those which are sufficiently overgrown that the branches of neighbouring trees touch. Dormice hate crossing open ground, especially dewy grass which would wet their fur. Leaving long branches for the dormice is a good excuse for skimping on the pruning!

In summer, dormice construct a spherical nest, typically of woven grass, honeysuckle bark and leaves. They may also use special wooden nest boxes, which resemble bird boxes but with the hole at the back to deter tits from using them. They need to be fixed low in suitable bushes. However, I have so far been unable to entice a grateful dormouse into the ones I put up for their express convenience. Instead, it seems that other small rodents find them a handy place for munching through my cobnuts, for when I clean them out each spring I find the boxes half full of empty nut shells.

A second species of dormouse, the edible dormouse, also occurs in Britain, but this one is not native. It was deliberately introduced to the wild at Tring Park, in Hertfordshire, in 1902, and from here it has spread into the neighbouring countryside. It is widely established on the Continent, and derives its name from the fact that the Romans used to eat it as a delicacy: it is much larger than our native dormouse. However, it is not so popular among all Italians now - Italy's hazel-nut industry is big business, and growers reckon that the dormice take up to 15% of their crop. In Britain it has also proved troublesome, stripping the bark off trees and killing them, and invading houses and chewing though wiring, drowning in water tanks, and making so much noise that it has been likened to a football team in the loft. Edible dormice even gnawed through organ pipes in a church. English cobnut growers hope they will never reach their orchards.

Red and Grey Squirrels

Today there are no wild red squirrels in south-east England, but nevertheless these animals do benefit from cobnuts. A man in Carlisle has for many years been supplementing the diet of local red squirrels with imported filberts. Unable to obtain sufficient supplies, he turned to Kentish cobnuts, introducing them mixed with the customary Italian hazel nuts in case they proved unpopular. Far from it - the cobnuts were selected and the filberts were left untouched by the discerning animals. The tonne of nuts sent to him annually is said to have greatly increased the squirrels' libido. Another customer finds that cobnuts are chosen when there is a choice of cobnuts and peanuts. Several people now purchase Kentish cobnuts for red squirrel food.

The first grey squirrels were introduced to Britain from America in 1876, others being imported and released until 1929. These attractive and amusing creatures have since spread through much of Britain, and have become a serious pest, replacing red squirrels, and damaging trees by stripping their bark. Research is in progress to find a contraceptive which can be fed to them in bait to control their numbers.

Raiding parties of grey squirrels visit nut plats in numbers not appreciated by the grower, their incessant chattering a maddening reminder of continuing depredations. They begin eating nuts as soon as the kernel starts to develop, which is typically not until early August, after the shell has grown to its full size. Until this stage is reached, the shell is filled by a woolly pith apparently of no interest to animals, with only a minute chit to indicate the future nut. At the last moment, the kernel grows incredibly fast to fill the shell completely within only two or three weeks. It is tempting to speculate that this rapid last-minute spurt of growth is a useful adaptation, minimising the period when the nut - the tree's seed - is attractive to the various animals which might eat it.

Squirrels can find trees with early-ripening nuts even when planted well within large orchards, and they soon strip them bare. The manufacturers of squirrel-proof bird feeders must be among the few to have benefited from the introduction of these disingenuously charming animals. The rest of Europe was not so foolish. Grey squirrels are found in only one place, in Italy, where they originated from four individuals released from a monastery soon after the last War; seemingly they were not all male, unlike the residents of the monastery, for they are spreading. They still only occupy an area of some two hundred square kilometres, although this is separated by little more than a large river from the main hazel nut growing region.

Red Squirrel
Illustration by Chris Embleton

Birds

Cobnut plats, with their lack of undergrowth and large nuts, are not particularly attractive to many kinds of birds, although the arrangement of small branches is suitable for the cup-shaped nests of blackbirds, thrushes and robins. However, cobnuts are greatly enjoyed by nuthatches, which seem unusually common in nut growing districts. The tap-tap-tap as they open a nut with their tough bill is a frequent sound in the season, and I do not resent the small number of nuts they take.

Sometimes the source of the tapping turns out to be not a nuthatch but a great tit. I have occasionally come across a nut securely wedged into a branch by these crafty birds, the shell opened and the kernel partly eaten and peppered with peck marks. As I complete my pruning in March, the strident twang of their call resounds through the plantation.

Wild Flowers

Old nut plantations often support an astonishingly rich and varied flora. Early spring brings a profusion of primroses *(illus. p.15)*; the best displays seem to be in lightly-grazed orchards. Moschatel also flowers early: it needs to, for it is only two or three inches high and is soon swamped by taller vegetation. Its alternative name of town hall clock arises from its curious green flowers, which are arranged cubically on the top of a stalk, like the four faces of Big Ben, with a fifth looking skywards *(illus. right)*.

Toothwort is another unusual species of early spring. It bears no leaves, for it is parasitic, deriving all its sustenance from the roots of the nut bush on which it lives. In March it sends up a sinister spike of fleshy pink flowers, which turn into a ghostly white seedhead. Toothwort is an uncommon plant, largely restricted to old woods and hedges, but once it has colonised a nut plat it seems to thrive. The populations growing in two commercial plats, near Maidstone where some 400 trees are affected, and another near Plaxtol, are thought to be the largest in the country. Luckily the plant seems not to reduce the number or quality of the nuts; presumably it draws insufficient nutrients from its host to cause significant damage. *(illus. p.20)*

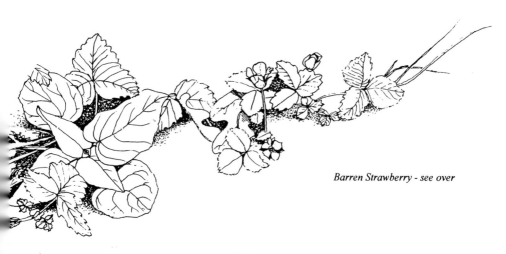

Barren Strawberry - see over

In early May one of my family's plats produces an uninterrupted sea of bluebells *(illus. p.16)*; it is now the best spread of bluebells in the neighbourhood since the nearby hornbeam woodland was cleared and replanted with conifers.

Barren strawberry *(illus. p.45)* grows under nut trees nearby. Its leaves and flowers so closely resemble the true wild strawberry that a close examination is required to confirm that there is no point in expecting any tasty red fruit.

Later on cow-wheat comes into flower. This is an uncommon plant of acid soils which is partly parasitic - it gains some of its nutrients from the roots of grasses.

Broad-leaved helleborine *(illus. p.19)*is the last species to bloom in my orchard, usually opening its curious green and pink flowers in July. This is the only plant I have discovered by touch. One evening I decided to gather a few last nuts in the twilight after some friends had left. My hand encountered a stiff stem bearing oval leaves, which I thought could only be those of this orchid, although, possessing no torch, I had eagerly to await the next morning to confirm my identification. The plant had missed the pre-harvest cut as it grows between two close-spaced trees, too narrow a gap for the mower. It has flowered in most years since then.

Tutsan, bugle, sanicle, wood spurge and bird's-nest *(illus. p.21)* and early purple orchids *(left)* are some of the interesting plants which can be found in plats on more calcareous soils.

46

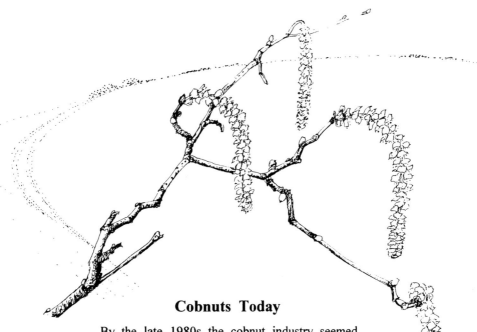

Cobnuts Today

By the late 1980s the cobnut industry seemed
close to extinction. I started to map and photograph
plats in the neighbourhood to retain some record of
what had once been there. Coincidentally, the European
Commission announced that grants were available for establishing
co-operatives for hazel nut growers. These were intended for
growers on the Continent, where nut cultivation is extensive, but
English growers were no less eligible. In fact the red tape dissuaded us from
applying, but we nevertheless set up an informal co-operative, the Kentish
Cobnuts Association, which has been so successful that cobnut cultivation is
thriving again, and even expanding. The Association has improved marketing
and promotion of nuts, and provides training. One important task is to keep
abreast of inappropriate legislation, usually emanating from the European
Community, such as the proposal to dry all hazel nuts before sale. That
would have led to the end of cobnut cultivation, for the very essence of
cobnuts is that they are fresh and unprocessed. Luckily, through the UK
government and with the help of the National Farmers Union, that proposal
was opposed successfully.

New orchards are being planted in Kent, as well as in other counties. Today's
supermarket requires nuts stripped of their husks, as they are considered more
attractive, or at any rate look more like the familiar imported filberts on sale
for Christmas. Kentish Cob's long husk is difficult to separate from the nut,
so short-husked varieties from abroad, such as Butler and Ennis, are

47

increasingly being planted in modern commercial plats. This trend can only accelerate as wholesale markets and high-street greengrocers decline; more than three quarters of fresh produce is now sold through supermarkets. However, Kentish Cob remains an excellent variety for those who are more interested in taste than look.

No more than about 250 acres of old plats survive, perhaps substantially fewer, and they continue to be lost to housing developments or for horse grazing. At present the attrition has slowed, and there is now recognition of their historical, cultural, wildlife and landscape value. Government grants are even available for restoration of derelict plats. Today many owners treasure their nut plats rather than seeing them as crooked old trees that should be cleared.

Nuts and Nutrition

'Nuts are notable not only for the superior quality of their protein but for their richness in lime, iron, and other mineral elements. Nuts are the quintessence of nutriment, in fact, the chef-d'oeuvre of Nature in food products. They supply for a given weight nearly twice the amount of nutriment of any other food product'.

Of course people have been enjoying hazel nuts long before Dr Kellogg penned this paean to nuts in 1932. It is likely that they formed a vital source of nutrition for prehistoric hunter-gatherer peoples, for whom their high fat content could well have been particularly important. Fat is a vital food, especially in winter when energy is required to keep warm. However, the meat of wild animals is lean at this season: they too are using up their bodily reserves accumulated during the summer and autumn. Hazel remains have also been found in many Mesolithic (10,000 to 4,500 years BCE) and later sites in Europe. In Britain, the remains of very large quantities of charred nutshells dating from the Mesolithic period have been found in a site on the island of Colonsay in the southern Hebrides. Collection of nuts may have been a communal activity, and it is possible that the nuts were then roasted. Roasted kernels keep well and were less bulky for nomadic peoples to carry

Nuts are just as nutritious to wildlife and in particular the Grey Squirrel is notorious for the acrobatics it will perform to get peanuts intended for the birds. A nut orchard is no more safe. This bird table scene is drawn from a photograph courtesy of David Elliott.

with them than unshelled nuts. They are also easier to grind into flour: ground food is easier to digest, and so is more nutritious.

Cobnut kernels typically contain 12%-17% protein by dry weight, and 10%-15% fibre. They are very rich in vitamin E and in calcium, typically containing 21mg and 141mg per 100g dry weight, respectively. They also provide about 0.4mg and 0.55mg of vitamins B1 and B6 respectively per 100g dry weight. Hazel nuts are fatty, with about 60% fat, which is more than peanuts and almonds but less than walnuts. However, only 5% is saturated fats, about the same as almonds and walnuts but much less than peanuts.

Cobnuts are mostly eaten fresh, either on their own or together with other ingredients, such as in a salad. Some people like to eat them with a little salt. If they are to be chopped, this is best done shortly before eating them, since they soon go rancid once they have been cut. Like many other fresh foods, cobnuts should be kept in the fridge, preferably in an open or part-covered container; the addition of some salt helps preserve them. To prevent mould they should not be allowed to sweat. If storing for more than a few days, loose husks should be removed, but it is not necessary to take off every one. Do not remove the husks if they are green and firmly attached to the nut. Ripe brown nuts can be kept for longer than the green nuts sold at the start of the season.

Many recipes using cobnuts require, or benefit from, the pre-roasting of the nuts. This greatly enhances their flavour, so that only a few ounces, coarsely ground, lend a nutty tang to recipes savoury or sweet. Place them in an oven at 300°F/150°C/Gas Mark 2 for up to an hour, depending on their size and freshness but shell them first! As a child I would sometimes throw nuts into bonfires, hoping they would explode, but at most only a disappointing muffled pop ensued. Putting them under a slow grill is faster, but be vigilant, as they blacken only a moment after they have reached the desired stage of being hard and brittle. About 4 oz (100g) nuts in their shells will produce 1½ oz (40g) of roasted kernels, but be generous - they are so delicious that some may never reach the dish.

RECIPES

Marrow stuffed with cobnuts and plums

Quantities for four:

1 large marrow or squash
2 medium onions, sliced thinly
2 cloves garlic (optional)
12 oz plums or 8 oz damsons
1 lb cobnuts (weighed in husk; less if they are rather dry)
6 oz mushrooms, sliced thickly
2 heaped teaspoons grated fresh root ginger
4 tomatoes, sliced
1 teaspoon mixed herbs
0.5 lb lean minced beef or lamb (optional)
Heat the oven to 325 °F, 170 °C, gas mark 3.

Wash the marrow or squash and split in half so that each half can be
stuffed.

Remove the seedy pith and place in an oven-proof dish.

Shell the cobnuts, chop coarsely.

Stone and halve the plums.

Fry the onion in a little butter for a few minutes.

Mix all the filling ingredients together,

Season to taste,

Pack into each half of the marrow,

Dot with a few knobs of butter.

Cover and cook for 1.5 to 2 hours,
depending on the size of the marrow.

Nutty Apple Ice

About a third of the dry weight of cobnut kernels is protein,
and there's the goodness of the apples,
so you can pretend this ice-cream is healthy eating!

1 lb cooking apples
1 tbsp water
peel of half a lemon cut into strips
1 tbsp lemon juice
4 oz (120g) sugar
2 eggs, separated
0.25 pt (150ml) each single and double cream
1.5 oz (40g) roasted cobnuts, coarsely ground

Cook the peeled apples with the water and lemon peel to a pulp in a
covered pan.

Sieve, add lemon juice, sugar and beaten egg yolks, and
leave to cool.

When cold, mix in the coarsely ground nuts, whip the
egg whites until stiff

Using the same whisk, whip the single and
double cream together.

First fold the cream into the apple mixture,
then the egg whites,

Freeze for two hours.

Cocoa nuts

Crack and shell some cobnuts, preferably keeping the kernel whole.

This is most easily achieved by cracking it end-on, if you have
suitable nut-crackers.

Roast the kernels until they are hard and
brown, but not black.

Soften a small quantity of dark chocolate in the bottom of a
saucepan, and roll the nuts in it until they are well coated.

Set aside on a plate to cool.

Sprinkle cocoa over them when the chocolate
is nearly set, turning them so they are coated all over.

This is an ideal treat for Christmas, as it is not too rich.

INDEX

Hazel nuts, Cobnuts, Filberts and Filbeards, together with their cultivar names occur throughout the book and are not indexed separately. Main topics are indexed below under Cobnuts. Writer's names are printed in italics.